BOOK ANALYSIS

Written by Leonie Cater

The Glass Menagerie

BY TENNESSEE WILLIAMS

BrightSummaries.com

TENNESSEE WILLIAMS

AMERICAN PLAYWRIGHT

- **Born in Columbus, Mississippi (United States) in 1911.**
- **Died in New York, New York (United States) in 1983.**
- **Notable works:**
  - *A Streetcar Named Desire* (1947), play
  - *Cat on a Hot Tin Roof* (1955), play
  - *Suddenly Last Summer* (1958), play

Amongst the most celebrated playwrights of 20th-century American drama, Tennessee Williams left his mark on literary history with his enthralling, tension-ridden oeuvre, dealing with themes as diverse and polemic as human sexuality, human relations and communications, homosexuality, social conventions and mental health. Several autobiographical details in his work have been identified and explored by critics, demonstrating that the writer drew on real life and his lived experiences in his creative processes. Parallels have been drawn, for example, between *The Glass Menagerie*'s Laura and Amanda Wingfield, and Williams' own sister and mother, respectively. It was this very play, in fact, that catapulted the playwright's career to the lofty heights of success, cementing his standing amongst such playwrights as Eugene O'Neill (1888-1953) and Arthur Miller (1915-2005). His career entered a period of steady decline later in life due to increased drug and alcohol use. This decrease in the popularity of his plays has also been attributed to Williams' attempt at a new style. He died on 25 February 1983 aged 71, having choked to death on a plastic bottle cap.

THE GLASS MENAGERIE

20TH-CENTURY AMERICAN DRAMA AND MEMORY PLAY

- **Genre:** play
- **Reference edition:** Williams, T. (2014) *The Glass Menagerie*. London: Penguin Modern Classics. Kindle Edition.
- **1st edition:** 1944
- **Themes:** memory, emotion, social conventions, gender divide, 1930s America, families

The Glass Menagerie marked the beginning of Williams' burgeoning career. Strongly autobiographical, the work was the writer's first success, cementing his position in literary history alongside the great playwrights of 20th-century American drama Eugene O'Neill (1888-1953) and Arthur Miller (1915-2005). Introduced to the audience as a 'memory play', the work is narrated by Tom Wingfield as he recounts his experiences with his overbearing mother and socially anxious sister. The era, we are told, is the 1930s, and thus the play takes places against a backdrop of rigid, oppressive social norms, as is the case with so many of Williams' plays. *The Glass Menagerie* has stood the test of time and is still performed in theatres and studied in classrooms all around the world today.

SUMMARY

SCENES ONE TO THREE

Curtains open to the set of a "lower middle-class" apartment (loc. 223). Glass animals (the 'menagerie') are visible to the audience, as is the photograph of the family's estranged patriarch and typewriting tools. Tom enters and begins his opening speech, setting the scene and historical context for the play: 1930s America. He describes the incoming characters: his mother (Amanda), sister (Laura) and the future "gentleman caller", as well as the looming photo of this father. Summoned to dinner by his mother, he is berated for his eating habits, giving the audience a sense of their antagonistic relationship. Laura remains nervously at the table while her mother besieges her with talk of potential "gentleman callers" – of which we learn Amanda herself once had plenty in her heyday, and of which Laura currently has none. Here, the audience first hears about the estranged father, the man whom Amanda picked from amongst this sea of potential suitors.

The next scene shows Laura in her own world, polishing her glass collection. Until her mother arrives, that is, and she jumps up to her desk to pretend to practise her typewriting skills. But to no avail: her mother has arrived to reveal that she has found out Laura's secret: she has not been attending business school as agreed, but instead has been wandering around parks and zoos for the past six weeks, having suffered a panic attack after her first 'speed test' during typewriting class. Amanda laments that the doomed destiny of the family hinges on Laura's inability to find a potential husband. Her daughter reveals that she did, in fact, once quite like one young man named Jim she met in high school – but that the last she heard of him, he was engaged. Amanda assures her daughter that she will marry one day too, which Laura is reluctant to believe.

Tom introduces scene three, describing the sequence of events following the revelation of Laura's lack of attendance at business school. His mother has become increasingly obsessed with finding a suitable husband for Laura. An argument takes place between mother and son, sparked by Amanda's disapproval of Tom's lifestyle and constant late-night attendance of the 'cinema', which she refuses to believe. She also accuses him of being selfish, a claim Tom resents in view of his work at the shoe warehouse to provide for the family. Tom calls her an "ugly - babbling old - witch..." (loc. 575) before attempting to storm out the door. His coat becomes caught and, frustrated, he hurls it across the room and, to Laura's horror, breaks his sister's glass menagerie. Amanda declares that she shall not speak to her son until he apologises, and she departs.

SCENES FOUR AND FIVE

The audience watches a drunken Tom stumble his way back home and up the fire escape to the apartment. He is greeted by his concerned sister, whom he calms with an absolutely unbelievable, longwinded story about his time at the movies, which the gullible Laura wholeheartedly believes. She goes on to implore her brother to resolve the quarrel between himself and their mother, which he is reluctant to agree to.

After a while, Laura leaves to go to the shops, leaving Tom and Amanda alone for the first time since their argument. Tom eventually apologises and Amanda bewails her extreme "devotion" (loc. 671) to her children and the negative effect of this. After a while, their conversation becomes tense again as Amanda harasses her son about his nightly attendance at the movies, his lack of commitment to his job and his growing resemblance to Mr Wingfield. She soon asks whether there are any "nice young men" (loc. 770) down at the warehouse where Tom is working and asks him to find a suitor for his sister. He reluctantly agrees and leaves for work.

Scene five opens with further hassling from Amanda towards her son, until the latter reveals the exciting news that he has, in fact, invited one of his work colleagues to dinner – and tomorrow. She interrogates Tom about the man – Jim – while Tom asks his mother not to put too much pressure on his sister or expect to much from her: she is "very different from other girls" (loc. 964), he explains.

SCENES SIX AND SEVEN

The time has come for Jim's arrival. Tom provides the audience with some background, explaining that Jim was a "high school hero" (loc. 452) who has somehow lost his way, ending up in a job that is not much better than Tom's own. When the lights come up on the Wingfield's living room, it is clear that Amanda has worked hard to make the place as presentable as possible, complete with a new floor lamp and new white curtains. Laura is in a new dress which is being adjusted by her mother, and soon Amada leaves the stage to appear in a fancy dress of her own, a "girlish frock" (loc. 1058) she wore to the cotillion and to receive her gentleman callers. Jim's name comes up in conversation between the pair and Laura becomes panicked as it becomes clear that this is the very same boy she liked in high school. She announces that she shall no longer be able to attend dinner and refuses to answer the door to Jim and her brother. Eventually she concedes and goes to greet the pair awkwardly before dashing away. Tom and Jim begin their own conversation, wherein Jim tells his friend to take his job more seriously, and in response Tom announces his desire and decision to leave the warehouse and his family to join the Union of Merchant Seamen.

It is soon time for dinner, but Laura faints before they can even begin eating and leaves to rest on the sofa. Jim stays with her while the other two return to wash the dishes and the pair strike up a conversation, Laura increasingly gaining confidence in his company as time goes on. Laura reveals that they knew each other in high school, reminding him of his nickname for her – Blue Roses – and he remembers, furthering their bond. Jim implores her not to be so shy and to take pride in her differences, to think of herself as "*superior* in some way" (loc. 1541). Encouraged, Laura introduces Jim to her glass menagerie and, in return, Jim invites her to dance. They waltz clumsily together around the room until they knock the table and break one of Laura's favourite pieces – the unicorn. She maintains her composure and Jim continues to inspire confidence in her, until, swept up in the moment, he kisses her. Moments later he remembers himself and apologises to Laura, explaining that he is actually "going steady" with another girl and will not be able to call again. With Laura now crushed anew, Amanda re-enters the living room with inappropriate gaiety for the current ambience. Jim makes his excuses and explains that he must be going to meet his girlfriend at the train station. Amanda wishes him farewell before turning on her son and accusing him of plotting to embarrass his family. Angered, Tom leaves for 'the movies' once again, leaving Laura and Amanda behind to console one another in the wake of the evening's events. In his closing speech, Tom reveals that, like his father before him, he did indeed abandon his family to go travelling, but has never been able to rid himself of the memory of Laura's face.

CHARACTER STUDY

TOM

Tom introduces himself to the audience as the play's narrator, the person whose memories are being played out on stage: "truth in the pleasant disguise of illusion." (loc. 248) As such, the play is introduced as the product of his imagination and therefore his creation, thus drawing an immediate parallel between the character and the work's playwright: if Tom is the creator of this fictional world we see before us, does that make him the playwright? This concept is reinforced by the various links between the life of the play's protagonist and that of Tennessee Williams himself. First and foremost, Thomas was Williams' own birth name, establishing an immediate, simple relation between the playwright and his protagonist. Secondly, we see many similarities between the two men's family lives. Williams, too, found himself in a monotonous, unsatisfying job in his early 20s (pushed by his father to start work at the International Shoe

Company factory); Williams, too, came from a broken family composed of a predominantly absent father, a mentally fragile sister and an overbearing mother.

As such, Tom is a rather complex character and the question of how to perceive his presentation is a difficult one. Indeed, at certain moments throughout the play, the audience feels sympathetic towards this frustrated poet, forced to provide for his difficult family and forget entirely about his dreams. When his mother chastises him for being selfish, Tom explodes with a passionate speech which truly rings home, pushing the audience to side with him: "For sixty-five dollars a month I give up all that I dream of doing and being ever!" he exclaims (loc. 559), "You think I'm in love with the Continental Shoemakers? You think I want to spend fifty-five years down there [...]!" (loc. 506). There *is*, however, a desire to be selfish inside of him, a desire which he gives into by the end of the play, paying his dues for the Union of Merchant Seamen instead of his family's electricity bill and abandoning them to begin his new life. The guilt Tom feels at this decision, however, is made evident by his confession that visions of

Laura follow him wherever he goes, triggered by anything from "a familiar bit of music" (loc. 1814) to a "piece of transparent glass" (loc. 1814). "Oh, Laura, Laura, I tried to leave you behind me, but I am more faithful than I intended to be!" he laments (loc. 1818). In this way, it would seem that the memory play is a series of recollections triggered by Tom's guilt over the way he treated his family, further demonstrated by the ultimately – surprisingly – sympathetic presentation of both his mother and sister.

AMANDA

Amanda is an archetypal Tennessee Williams character: the former Southern belle desperate to reclaim her former economic and social glory, a type echoed in *A Streetcar Named Desire*'s Blanche Dubois and Maggie in *Cat on a Hot Tin Roof*. Amanda's former beauty and social standing is made clear in her introductory scene, where she waxes lyrical about the influx of suitors she received in her heyday, boasting to her children that, "One Sunday afternoon in Blue Mountain – your mother received – seventeen! – gentlemen callers!" (loc. 303) It is evident that this is a common topic of conversation amongst the Wingfield family, signalled by Tom's anticipation of the story ("I know what's coming!", loc. 298) and Laura's confirmation: "Yes. But let her tell it [...] She loves to tell it" (loc. 301). It therefore becomes clear that Amanda prefers to evoke and live in the past, further demonstrated by her choice of attire when Jim comes to visit: a "girlish frock of yellowed voile" (loc. 1058), the very same dress in which she "led the cotillion" (loc. 1059) and "won the cakewalk twice" (loc. 1060) she explains to her audience "feverishly" (loc. 1059). In this way, along with her outdated, offensive references to "niggers" (loc. 302) and "darkies" (loc. 292), Amanda comes to embody the nostalgia of the Deep South for a more economically prosperous time, regardless of the slavery and antiquated views about women the previous era entailed.

While initially presented as an antagonistic character due to her constant, seemingly unfair hassling of Tom, by the end of the play her good intentions become clear. Indeed, having been subjected to the social and economic implications of living in a father-less, husband-less household in the 1930s, Amanda is simply doing everything in her power to set matters to rights. Nonetheless, she continues to play into contemporary social conventions, attempting to mould her son into the man her husband could never be and her daughter into an eligible, younger version of herself. The final scene demonstrates the genuine care she feels for her children, as she takes her daughter into her arms and consoles her: "Now that we cannot hear the mother's speech, her silliness is gone and she has dignity and tragic beauty [...] Amanda's gestures are slow and graceful, almost dancelike, as she comforts her daughter" (loc. 1805). Through Amanda's character progression, we can perhaps chart the emotional effect of Tom's memory: as our protagonist and narrator begins to feel deeper shame and guilt over his abandonment of the family, the presentation of his mother becomes increasingly sympathetic.

LAURA

Beleaguered by social anxiety and lacking in any purpose other than the maintenance of her cherished glass menagerie, Laura is described by her brother as being "very different from other girls" (loc. 964), "terribly shy" (loc. 967) and "a little peculiar" (*ibid.*). She lives under the direction of her mother and the only rebellion we see against this is her lack of attendance at the business school she was supposedly enrolled in, due to her extreme social anxiety. The nervous dispositions of both Amanda and Laura are the apparent result of contemporary social pressures and conventions, the two women being dependent on a father and husband who is absent, a son and brother who seemingly does not care, and potential gentleman callers who do not exist. They are powerless at the hands of the fate society has prepared for them.

Like her mother, the portrayal of Laura's character is not constant throughout the play. She undergoes a major transformation under the temporary influence of the family's long-awaited gentleman caller, Jim, who assures her of the importance of being "different" (loc. 1648). Despite her initial, tongue-tied awkwardness, Laura becomes increasingly confident in her interactions with her former crush and current visitor Jim, allowing herself to be swept up into a waltz with this near-stranger and even be kissed on the lips. The spell is broken and her hopes are dashed, however, when Jim reveals that he is "going steady" (loc. 1690) with a girl named Betty, leaving Laura with a "look of almost infinite desolation" (loc. 1704). By allowing Jim's revelation to dramatically curtail Laura's dramatic transformation, Williams reflects and highlights the impact and power of the male over the female in 1930s American South.

ANALYSIS

STRINGS ATTACHED

The respective situations and fates of each main character in *The Glass Menagerie* are particularly dark and limited, a common theme throughout Williams' plays. Indeed, as Desmond Reid helpfully explains in his article *Tennessee Williams*:

> "The characters which Tennessee Williams puts before us are people in trouble [...] Sometimes he crowds all the trouble on to the shoulders of one unhappy person; sometimes there are two or three, equally unhappy, whose lives and troubles intermingle; sometimes he leaves them at the curtain-fall with a dim ray of hope; more often there is none." (1957: 432)

In this case, we see 'two or three equally unhappy' characters, each with no way out: even when Tom manages to apparently escape his predicament, he is plagued by ghostly memories of his hopeless sister, harassed by his own guilt.

Such inescapable unhappiness is presented as being symptomatic of a society ruled over by conventions and discrimination, the women being trapped in their dependence on their male counterparts, and the men being restricted by this very dependence. Amanda has been abandoned by her husband, and therefore by her primary source of income, leading to her social and economic decline, which is made all the more devastating by the importance she places on her own standing and former glories; Laura is brimming with insecurities born of a society which marginalises those seen as mentally or physically impaired, and with dismay resulting from her inability to comply with society's demands that she find a husband as soon as possible; Tom is forced to abandon his dreams and provide for his family in a job he despises. In this way, all three characters have had their wings clipped by an overbearingly discriminatory, misogynistic society, which begs the question: is Williams highlighting these social injustices, or using them as a base from which to explore human emotion and unhappiness?

MEMORY VERSUS REALITY

Biographical links have been made between Williams' life and other plays – Stanley Kowalski of *A Streetcar Named Desire*, for example, is based on a man Williams met during his time working at a shoe factory – but these references to his lived experiences are most purposeful and self-conscious in *The Glass Menagerie*. As previously discussed, the home life of Tom almost directly mirrors that of Williams' early life and, from the outset of the play, Williams seeks to highlight the importance of the work's nature as a 'memory play'. In the opening stage directions, the playwright writes, "Memory takes a lot of poetic license. It omits some details; others are exaggerated, according to the emotional value of the articles it touches, for memory is seated predominantly in the heart" (loc. 228). In this way, the audience is immediately alerted to the play's innate subjectivity, and it becomes a challenge to identify what truly happened in the incidences being remembered by Tom.

As such, the events themselves as they occur on stage are of secondary importance to the emotions evoked and represented therein, for this is the true key to understanding our protagonist. When Amanda appears in her girlish frock to greet Jim, for example, what matters is not whether the costume has been exaggerated for comedic effect or impact, but rather what this signifies regarding Tom's impression of his mother – and therefore Tennessee William's recollection of his own. This is also the case when Tom goes on his impassioned diatribes about his frustration at working in the shoe factory, and at being under the hawk-like direction of his mother, exclaiming excitedly:

> "TOM: I'm going to opium dens! Yes, opium dens, dens of vice and criminals' hangouts, Mother. I've joined the Hogan Gang, I'm a hired assassin, I carry a tommy gun in a violin case! I run a string of cat houses in the Valley! They call me Killer, Killer Wingfield, I'm leading a double-life, a simple, honest warehouse worker by day, by night a dynamic czar of the underworld, Mother." (loc. 568)

In these speeches, what matters is not precisely what he is saying – it would be impossible for Tom to recall the exact content of his entire speech – but the impassioned energy behind those words. Symbolism is key to Williams' oeuvre – but in *The Glass Menagerie*, the words and actions themselves become the symbols, existing as indications of Tom's mindset rather than as genuine, accurate events in themselves.

SYMBOLISM IN THE SET

Each of Williams' choices regarding set, costume and props is dripping with symbolism – but two main focal points are Laura's glass menagerie and the portrait of Mr Wingfield, the play's "fifth character" (loc. 259), two diametrically opposed props considering their symbolism. Tom tells us in his introductory lines that his father "doesn't appear except in this larger-than-life-size photograph over the mantel" (*ibid.*) and that he was a "telephone man who fell in love with long distances; he gave up his job with the telephone company and skipped the light fantastic out of town" (loc. 260). The last thing they received from him was a postcard from Mexico with no address. Mr Wingfield's absence is a paradoxically strong presence, with both Amanda and Tom constantly referring to the missing patriarch: the former with regret, the latter with longing to live the same existence, free from these family ties. And when Tom is lamenting his situation to his sister, he ponders, "You know it don't take much intelligence to get yourself into a nailed-up coffin, Laura. But who in hell ever got himself out of one without removing one nail?" (loc. 621) and "as if in answer, the father's grinning photograph lights up" (loc. 623). In this way, the portrait comes to symbolise both the continued impact of the patriarch, and the male's relatively free existence in comparison to his female counterparts: Tom may be restrained, but at least he has the choice to leave – a choice he ultimately makes.

In contrast, Laura's glass menagerie comes to symbolise fragility and imprisonment. Just as her own delicate, glass animals are stuck in one position and confined to the locations allocated by their owner, the sensitive Laura is constricted by the expectations both of society and her mother, perhaps explaining her affinity and attachment to these immobile creatures. Taking this symbolism even further, one could argue that the glass menagerie comes to represent the entire household, explaining the play's title. Indeed, not just Laura but the entire household is of a relatively nervous disposition, easily angered or upset by familial tensions, reflecting the delicate nature of Laura's glass animals. And it is not just Laura who feels the restrictive reins of contemporary social conventions, but Tom and Amanda also. In this way, the glass menagerie may be seen as a reflection of the Wingfield family as a whole.

FURTHER REFLECTION

SOME QUESTIONS TO THINK ABOUT...

- What do you make of Amanda's use of offensive and derogatory terms for African Americans? Is Williams criticising the enduring racism of the Deep South?
- How would you stage the play in a modern context?
- Tom is the play's narrator, but is he actually the play's protagonist?
- What has actually been keeping Tom from following his dreams until this point? Is it really just a matter of guilt and familial love?
- Is there anything you gain from reading the play that you would lose in watching it being performed?
- What similarities can you perceive between *The Glass Menagerie* and any other Tennessee Williams plays you have read?

We want to hear from you!
Leave a comment on your online library
and share your favourite books on social media!

FURTHER READING

REFERENCE EDITION

- Williams, T. (2014) *The Glass Menagerie*. London: Penguin Modern Classics. Kindle Edition.

REFERENCE STUDIES

- (No date) Tennessee Williams. *Encyclopaedia Britannica*. [Online]. [Accessed 30 November 2018]. Available from: <https://www.britannica.com/biography/Tennessee-Williams>
- Reid, D. (1957) Tennessee Williams. *An Irish Quarterly Review*. 46(184).
- Roudané, M. C. (1997) *The Cambridge Companion to Tennessee Williams*. Cambridge: Cambridge University Press.

ADAPTATIONS

- *The Glass Menagerie*. (1950) [Film] Irving Rapper. Dir. USA: Warner Bros.
- *The Glass Menagerie*. (1987) [Film] Paul Newman. Dir. USA: Cineplex Odeon Films.

MORE FROM BRIGHTSUMMARIES.COM

- Reading guide – *Cat on a Hot Tin Roof* by Tennessee Williams.
- Reading guide – *A Streetcar Named Desire* by Tennessee Williams.

www.brightsummaries.com

Ebook EAN: 9782808016667

Paperback EAN: 9782808016674

Legal Deposit: D/2018/12603/595

Cover: © Primento

Digital conception by Primento, the digital partner of publishers.

Printed in Great Britain
by Amazon

35479345R10029